FASHIONS OF A
DECADE
THE
1990s

FASHIONS OF A DECADE
THE 1990s

Elane Feldman

Series Editors: Valerie Cumming and Elane Feldman
Original Illustrations by Robert Price

Facts On File®

Contents

Facts On File, Inc.
11 Penn Plaza
New York NY 10001

Facts On File books are available at special discounts when purchased in bulk quantities for businesses, associations, institutions or sales promotions. Please call our Special Sales Department in New York at 212/967-8800 or 800/322-8755.
You can find Facts On File on the World Wide Web at http: // www. factsonfile.com

Text design by Christine Bell
Jacket design by Lisa Morris
Composition by Latimer Trend
Manufactured through World Print Ltd
Printed in Hong Kong

10 9 8 7 6 5 4 3

This book is printed on acid-free paper.

Library of Congress Cataloging-in-Publication Data
Feldman, Elane.
   Fashions of a decade. The 1990s / Elane Feldman : series editors.
   Valerie Cumming and Elane Feldman : original illustrations by Robert Price
      p.   cm.
   Includes bibliographical references and index.
   Summary: Explores, through text and illustrations, how fashions and clothes reflect the social, political, and cultural climate of their time.
   ISBN 0–8160–2472–3
   1. Fashion—United States—History—20th century—Juvenile literature.   2. Costume—United States—History—20th century––Juvenile literature.   3. United States—Social life and customs—20th century—Juvenile literature.   4. United States––Politics and government—20th century—Juvenile literature.
   [1. Costume—History—20th century.   2. Fashion—History—20th century.   3. Civilization, Modern—20th century.]   I. Cumming, Valerie.   II. Price, Robert, ill.   III. Title.   IV. Title: 1990s.
GT615.F45   1992
391'.009'049—dc20   92–8887

THE 90s

As the 1990s began, intense winds of change were sweeping over the globe. In many ways the very face of the world was altered as the 21st century approached. The nations of Eastern Europe demanded independence from almost a half-century of domination by the USSR. The Communist hold on Eastern Europe crumbled. Under the leadership of the USSR's

Mikhail Gorbachev, a proponent of *glasnost* (openness) and *perestroika* (restructuring), the last decade of the 20th century began with the 40-year-old Berlin Wall, dividing East and West Germany, tumbling. In October 1990, Germany was officially reunited. Demonstrations and the demands of the people produced radical changes in the Eastern European governments. In Romania, beginning in early

1990, public demonstrations took place that criticized the country's new leadership and also protested the large number of ex-Communists in the provisional regime. When Soviet Foreign Minister Eduard Shevardnadze visited Romania, he announced that Moscow would support any political system that emerged. This was a remarkable change in a country that had suffered for nearly one-quarter of a

5

century under the brutal reign of dictator Nicolae Ceausescu. He, and his wife, had fled in late 1989 – they were subsequently pursued, tried and executed for the crimes of theft, genocide and abuse of power.

Meanwhile, the Bulgarian National Assembly voted to repeal that portion of their constitution that guaranteed the Communists a dominant role as the sole political party in the country. Hungary declared itself to be a free republic. In Czechoslovakia, the first free elections in over 40 years were held. Popular hero and dissident playwright Vaclav Havel's Civic Forum Party and its allies were victors in the national parliamentary elections. Havel had said: ''We want democracy, we want to join the European Community, we want social justice and a free market economy. We may be socialists, but without these things there can be no socialism.'' Yet, even with the new-found freedom from Soviet domination, unrest was evident. At a rally in Bratislava, hundreds of people heckled him chanting: ''Enough of Havel! Enough of Prague! Independence for Slovakia.'' Havel called for a nationwide referendum to decide the future of the Czechoslovak federation.

Even in remote Mongolia, a barren land situated between the People's Republic of China and the Soviet Union, changes were felt. The Communist Party's local general secretary announced that the Party would work with others to seek political reform and they voted to drop its constitutional monopoly on power. In his book *The Shattered Bloc* Elie Abel comments, ''. . . [even] the term Eastern European has fallen out of favor.

Top: **End of an era. A statue of Lenin is removed from public display in Moscow after the unsuccessful coup by hard-line Communists in August 1991.**

Bottom: **Wild celebrations as the two Germanies become one again. But the practical problems of uniting two countries would be with the new Germany for some time.**

Toward a closer Europe. Breakthrough, as workers digging both sides of the Channel Tunnel linking France and England join up.

Large numbers of Poles, Hungarians, Czechs and Slovaks, Slovenes and Croats object to being labeled as Eastern Europeans. They prefer to [be known as] Central Europeans." Political observers pointed out that, with the USSR's severe shortages of consumer items and food, the Soviet's "external empire" had to be dismantled.

In February of 1990 there were huge (and previously unheard of) "prodemocracy" demonstrations in over 30 Soviet cities. Then on May Day that year, at the traditional parade in Moscow's Red Square – for the first time in decades – an independent and unofficial group of marchers appeared proclaiming their belief in ethnic nationalism.

In mid-1991, in a dramatic turn of events, Boris Yeltsin easily won the Russian republic's presidential election, capturing 60 percent of the votes. Even with a strong showing from the Communists, the Russian voters overwhelmingly elected Yeltsin, who was a vocal champion of decentralization and democratization. This was in the republic that made up three-fourths of

A New Europe?

In Europe a new age was heralded with the coming in 1992 of the "Single Market" within the European Economic Community. The EEC itself had existed since 1958 – its founder members comprised Belgium, France, Germany, Italy, Luxembourg and the Netherlands. Denmark, Great Britain, Greece, Ireland, Portugal and Spain had all joined subsequently. The "Single Market" was intended to merge the economies of these dozen countries into one market, with an estimated 340 million consumers – with coordinated product standards and tax structures, as well as the existing free passage of goods, capital, services and people. Many people felt that this new "United States of Europe" would mean that nations would finally overcome centuries of rivalry, and sometimes outright armed conflict. It was felt that language barriers and cultural differences would diminish and all would benefit from the economic, military, cultural and commercial effects of the "one Europe."

However, many outside observers were dubious and expressed grave concern that a so-called Single Market Europe would actually create a "fortress Europe." In Great Britain, conversely, concerns were loudly voiced in varied ways, including the adamant reluctance of many to have the British nation entirely give up sterling as a monetary unit in favor of a single European currency. However, the long-awaited Channel Tunnel, linking Britain and France (which had first been proposed almost 200 years before), provided clear evidence of Britain's increasingly strong ties with Continental Europe.

Patriotic fashions abounded in the wake of the Gulf War. This Stars-and-Stripes T-shirt is teamed with red tights.

the Soviet Union and represented half its people.

In August 1991, in Moscow, conservative Communists mounted an unsuccessful coup, attempting to restore the power of the Communist Party and to keep the Soviet empire intact. It succeeded, however, only in revealing the weakness of the central government, leading to many of the Soviet Republics ultimately declaring their total independence. (These included Latvia, Lithuania, and Estonia.) By late 1991 worldwide headlines blared the news of the dismantling of the entire structure of Soviet communism.

Going Through Changes

In Central America, in Nicaragua – which had been under the leadership of the Soviet-supported Sandinistas since 1979 – changes also took place. President Daniel Ortega was

defeated by Violeta Arrios de Chamorro, who belonged to no political party. The Soviets had indicated to Ortega that they were no longer able to help the Nicaraguan revolution.

But it was not only in the Communist and allied nations that changes were felt. In February 1990 the South African government released the nationalist, anti-apartheid activist Nelson Mandela after 27 years in jail.

Elsewhere on the political scene the USA's George Bush, who had replaced two-term Republican President Ronald Reagan in 1988, was widely quoted for his affirmation that his would be an administration leading "a kinder, gentler nation." The sentiment behind this statement was welcomed by the huge numbers of impoverished and homeless Americans, and millions of other people concerned about these groups.

Domestic "gentleness" aside, President Bush acted firmly in January

Bush, the USA and its allies were also victors in the Gulf War.

1991, spearheading the United Nations forces that repelled the invading Iraqi army from its "incursion" into Kuwait. The Iraqi incursion resulted in armed conflict with civilian and military losses for the participants. This conflict (which was referred to as the Gulf War) sparked anti-war demonstrations. But at the same time, a huge outpouring of patriotic support was shown for the troops sent to the Gulf. People across America tied yellow ribbons around trees and lampposts, (as in the song "Tie a Yellow Ribbon 'Round the Old Oak Tree"); doing so had come to signify support for the troops on the home front, and, to many, a pledge not to forget the soldiers until all were home. People also began wearing flag and other patriotically embellished apparel, which were quickly offered for sale.

Fashions Go International

As the world shrunk, fashions criss-crossed international boundaries with rapidity. The distinctive "American look" continued to command attention, as exemplified by well-known U.S. designers such as Ralph Lauren, Calvin Klein, Bill Blass and Donna Karan. A further group of highly praised, young designers, including Michael Kors, Norma Kamali, Carmelo Pomodoro, Isaac Mizrahi and Gordon Henderson, also made international fashion headlines. The American Oscar de la Renta, in a break with fashion practice, showed his fall 1991 collection in Paris, even before doing so in New York City. The expensive gamble paid off and, by the next fashion season, de la Renta was accepted as being part of the "Paris collection scene," and his orders tripled from those of the previous year.

"The latest buzzword for fashion isn't mini or maxi or stretch. It's globalization" reported Anne-Marie Schiro in the *New York Times*. American manufacturers, designers and retailers in seeking new markets began to look toward tapping the $50 billion women's European ready-to-wear market. U.S. labels such as Calvin Klein, de la Renta, Karan and Adrienne Vittadini could already be found in European stores. And American retail stores such as The Gap, The Limited and Esprit had opened in England; Barney's and Charivari opened in Japan.

Calvin Klein told Ms. Schiro: ". . . Europe wants American clothes, and America needs Europe . . . the goal is

***Right:* A striking Arnold Scaasi black-and-white outfit, worn with an outsize brim hat.**

The Fight Against Disease

Medical science promised long-sought solutions to many of humankind's ills. In mid-1991, researchers at New York City's Albert Einstein College of Medicine, Howard Hughes Institute, announced a vital step toward the development of an all-important "multi-disease" vaccine that could, with a single dose, provide immunity against wide-ranging diseases, including: tuberculosis, tetanus, diphtheria, Lyme disease, measles, hepatitis, malaria, other parasitic diseases and some forms of cancer. The journal *Nature* reported that the technique developed might also be applicable to finding and creating an AIDS vaccine. According to one of the scientists, Dr. Barry Bloom, "such a multi-disease vaccine could save millions of lives, particularly those of children in the Third World."

In other groundbreaking work, a group of UCLA (University of California at Los Angeles) School of Medicine neurosurgeons announced in 1990 a method for delivering cancer-fighting agents to brain tumor cells without injury to normal brain cells, by selectively opening the blood-brain barrier directly in the tumor. Also, UCLA researchers, along with those at the University of Texas Health Science Center in San Antonio, announced a major step in identifying a specific gene that probably plays an important role in causing alcoholism. The study was the first to demonstrate a specific genetic association to alcoholism, a disease that for centuries had afflicted millions throughout the world.

In late 1991, immunologists from the Ludwig Institute for Cancer Research, in Brussels, Belgium, reported the discovery of a long-searched-for tumor antigen. (An antigen is a substance that stimulates production of an antibody when introduced into a living organism.) Such a substance would help to create a cancer vaccine to marshal the body's immune system to either destroy a tumor or to prevent the recurrence of cancer, once an initial malignancy had been removed. While the Belgian results were reported as being "extremely preliminary," they were enthusiastically greeted in the field of cancer research.

"By the time you finish reading this magazine, AIDS will have emptied all of these."

– Kenneth Cole

The campaign to warn the public of the dangers of the AIDS virus continued to produce many moving and effective posters, such as this one.

As the decade progressed, scores of other scientific finds and explorations held hope that in the 21st century humankind would live longer and healthier lives. The coming of the millennium augured well for the resolution of many medical mysteries that had long plagued humankind.

to have shops in all the major cities to showcase what I do, and then to more widely distribute the less expensive line.'' Mr. Klein also remarked that while some European retailers visited New York City to view designer collections, less expensive lines of apparel needed to be taken to the overseas buyers to widen distribution.

In 1992, to do just this and to help small American manufacturers penetrate the global market, the United States Commerce Department sponsored national participation at a number of Asian and European fashion trade shows. In February 1992, with the help of the U.S. Embassy in Paris, there was, for the first time, an American Design Pavillion at the important *Prêt-à-Porter Feminin* (women's ready-to-wear show) in Paris. It featured several dozen apparel and accessories designers who weren't large enough to enter the European market without help.

American mail order merchants were also moving into overseas markets. In late 1991, a dozen mail order companies collaborated on a catalog offering typically American products, initially to some 50,000 Japanese consumers. The cover of the catalog, called *American Showcase* (with text printed in Japanese), featured a photo of a blonde-haired, blue-eyed woman peeking over a Japanese-style hand fan picturing an American flag.

"Color Blocking" made fashion news in the early nineties. From America's "Gantos" by Issues came this color-blocked leisure outfit.

Right: **A clinging minidress by Thierry Mugler that embodies all the freedom and sensuality of early nineties dance and evening wear.**

George Rosenbaum, president of the Chicago market research firm Leon J. Shapiro & Associates, explained, ''The Japanese are hungry for a certain kind of Americana.'' The catalog contained a significant number of just such items: many in denim, and also accessories such as silver-plated bolo ties (the thin string tie worn by cowboys), cowboy boots, and even a (costly for mail order merchandise) $1,400 lambskin blazer.

The USA's couture designer, Arnold Scaasi – often referred to by the single name Scaasi – also drew worldwide attention, creating custom-made garments for First Lady Barbara Bush. This added to his already considerable prestige as dressmaker to some of the world's best-dressed and news-making women. Ms. Bush's style was itself of news value. She was decidedly unlike her predecessor, the controversial Nancy Reagan, who was always attired in the latest, most expensive high-fashion outfits and accessories. Ms. Bush favored a more relaxed, traditional, down-to-earth, but always correct and comfortably fashionable, understated style. Her preference for wearing her ''fake'' (costume) pearl necklace, created by self-proclaimed international ''King of Junk Jewelry,'' the American Kenneth Jay Lane, helped spur a renewed interest in wearing such necklaces. Even when dressed in her magnificent Scaasi ballgown for her husband's presidential inauguration she wore the famed ''fake'' pearls!

A sleek silver anorak with hood by Louis Feraud encapsulates the continuing sportswear influence.

France's Louis Feraud also created boldly printed garments, including these sophisticated silk walking shorts, with camisole and jacket.

The underwear theme as interpreted by Thierry Mugler in Paris.

Where once it was Paris alone that dictated fashion trends and "acceptable" styles, by the 1990s, the Parisian influence continued to be diluted. Designers working in Italy and the United Kingdom along with those in America contributed to the international look of fashion. In the U.K. the stylings of Vivenne Westwood, Zandra Rhodes, Rifat Ozbek, Richard Nott, Joe Casely-Hayford and Graham Fraser drew international attention. In Italy the Missonis and Fendis, as well as the prolific Giorgio Armani and the innovative Franco Moschino and Dolce-Gabanna team, continued to attract fashion editors' attention. There was also a renewed interest in the house of Pucci. This was understandable, given the company's role as the creator of the vividly patterned and colored prints identified with the 1960s, many of which were returning to vogue along with other "retro" stylings popular early in the 1990s.

Above left and right: America's Isaac Mizrahi attracted attention with his bold unmatched jackets, skirts and trousers.

Right: Temporary tattoos enjoyed a brief fad on the club scene.

Left: Underwear-inspired outerwear, from Mariella Burani of Italy.

Goodbye to the Yuppies

In the 1980s, thousands of people had feverishly pursued the "high life," spending large sums of money on luxury cars and homes and on costly dinners at fancy restaurants. American writer Tom Wolfe's best-selling book *Bonfire of the Vanities* painted a vivid picture of this 1980s yuppie lifestyle carried to the extreme. The 1990s, however, began on a bleaker note.

As the nineties dawned, a deepening economic recession, and high unemployment figures, meant that for large numbers of people the previous decade's freewheeling spending came to a screeching halt. The darkening economic picture produced far-ranging effects. Fewer people were dining out at high priced eateries. At-home entertainment replaced costly nights out. Rentals of home videos soared. A national survey carried out in the USA conducted in 1991 by the Hobby Industry Association found that 77 percent of U.S. households held at least one crafts hobbyist – this represented a 13 percent increase over the previous year. Book publishers also reported increased sales of books on crafts.

As people tightened their purse strings and closed their checkbooks, retail sales of all types of merchandise faltered. Manufacturers and retailers of apparel were particularly hard hit. Fashion shops and departments in large stores – especially those catering to working and middle-class people – showed significantly reduced revenues. Sales of all types, offering merchandise at deeply discounted prices, were widely seen.

New Sales Patterns

Rather than holding seasonal clearance sales, many retailers – mindful of shoppers' cautious buying habits – responded by offering nearly year-round sales of new, seasonal merchandise. Some retailers also had to rethink their sales philosophies. Once, for example, the junior department at major stores carried merchandise for younger women at about a tenth of the price of designer collections. One new pattern that emerged in the nineties was that increasingly these junior departments paid more attention to stocking what is referred to as "fashion forward" – i.e., more stylish, often quite *avant garde*, styles. The chief executive of major American manufacturer The Gillian Company Jon Levy was quoted as saying: "It used to be chic to tell your friends how much you spent on your clothes. Now you hear people at parties bragging that they didn't spend that much."

The seventies revival. Georgia Robinson models her own revamping of flares and gold chains.

20

Norma Kamali follows both the influences of biker leathers and the exotic east.

A New Diffusion

Top-of-the-line designers recognized the changing buying patterns and took action. John Galliano, once called, ''the spiritual leader of the British fashion business,'' launched a less expensive ''Galliano Girl'' collection in 1991. These items sold for about one-half the price of his other garments and were styled to attract a younger buyer. (These more affordable garments were originally known in Europe as ''diffusion'' collections.)

In 1987, British designer Rifat Ozbek had created a small collection of T-shirts, under the ''Future Ozbek'' label. Ozbek's shirts reflected his Turkish heritage and were particularly popular in Italy. These influences – of the Mideast and the Mediterranean – inspired the ethnic look of his earliest ''Future Ozbek'' clothing, with heavy embroidery becoming one of his signature styles. By the early 1990s Ozbek had gained wide popularity in London and elsewhere. In his 1990 collection he urged the ''staid'' London fashion scene to ''Release It,'' and for fall his garments were street

The Italian Way

In 1991, the Italian apparel manufacturer Compagnia Internazionale Abbigliamento undertook production of several less expensive collections for American designers, including Michael Kors. As the company produced its own fabrics and owned its own factories, they were able to manufacture quality garments at below one-half the price of designer clothes.

inspired – reflecting the clothing that was hot among the "club kids" of London and New York. This translated into bright colored garments aglitter with sequins or made of lush velvet. He also showed short, flippy skirts worn over black tights, and bustiers and dresses that emphasized the wearer's body. His spring 1991 collection carried an African theme, with use of a triangular African motif. Ozbek favored practical cotton in vivid tones of red, orange, yellow and white – as well as denims in orange, purple-brown, glowing greens and yellow. Many of the cottons were what Ozbek called "deck chair styles" – wide

stripes of color, or gray-white striped, stretch chambray.

Ozbek wasn't the only European who created less costly collections. Italy's Franco Moschino, under his "Cheap & Chic" label, also designed less expensive apparel. Moschino favored using cream-colored fabrics, to avoid the "glare" of dead white; and his earliest stylings in these collections included those bearing his signature question mark print, hot pants, and amusingly shaped buttons, as well as Pop Art inspired fabrics. Other noted designers from the United States, the United Kingdom, Italy and France also created less costly, secondary collec-

tions. These included: Great Britain's Jean Muir; America's Donna Karan, Calvin Klein, Adrienne Vittadini, Bill Blass and Geoffrey Beene; and on the Continent: Sonia Rykiel, Mario Valentino, Jean-Paul Gaultier, Giorgio Armani, Gianfranco Ferre, and Emanuel Ungaro.

The less expensive garments were no longer ignored by the fashion editors. *Vogue* magazine, for example, devoted pages to inexpensive clothes. The message was not lost on scores of designers who had watched the success of the secondary lines created by these talents. American designer-manufacturer Donna Karan,

Right: **A layered minidress from John Galliano's fall 1991 collection. Galliano was another designer to move his base of operations (from London to Rome) in order to "internationalize" his clientele.**

Below: **Ozbek also used vinyl as a fabric – a choice that was popular among many designers in the early nineties. This design typifies international "club wear" of the period.**

Above: **Boldly colored styles for men – and women – from Jean-Paul Gaultier. Not all men were intent on reinterpreting classic suit styles.**

Left: **African motifs from Rifat Ozbek.**

hailed as "the Princess of 7th Avenue" (the New York City street central to the garment trade), was someone who was closely watched. Ms. Karan enjoyed success with her "DKNY" line of apparel, priced below her more costly garments. American designers increasingly took to creating secondary, less expensive collections. One popular young American designer, Michael Kors, was quoted as saying, "Just because a woman doesn't have the pocketbook, doesn't mean she doesn't have style." Designer Anna Sui agreed, "I never felt a woman should pay every penny she earns to be stylish. People from the eighties who wanted the best of everything are spending more wisely now." Other designers cut costs in varied ways. Ronaldus Shamask canceled his fall 1991 show and kept garment details to a minimum. He also used only American fabrics. He said, "We're trying to create more value."

Menswear Plays It Safe – in the Main

Save for young and more adventuresome males, men's fashions in the 1990s were quiet interpretations on classic themes. Styles were mostly traditional: solid and pinstriped suitings, subdued checks and plaids, and ties and other accessories similar to those worn by 1980s men. Some men, however, struck a bolder note – especially for leisure time. Bright vests were seen on some; others, particularly those working in creative fields, favored unusual outfits, including T-shirts under their jackets. In the U.S. many young, mainly inner-city males emulated the "macho" rapper style of dressing, as worn by popular rap music performers, including M. C. Hammer.

After the Wall Came Tumbling Down

With the collapse of the Communist bloc, not only did those nations previously cut off from the fashion mainstream experience a free (including fashion) press, but savvy entrepreneurs stepped forward. In the USA a mail order company produced a "Russian Dressing" catalog, whose cover proclaimed it contained, "Crafts & collectibles from the USSR & Eastern Europe [and that] 10 percent of proceeds from sales would be donated to groups cleaning Eastern Europe's environment and to strengthening U.S.–Soviet ties." The catalog offered an unusual array of items including an "authentic Russian navy tunic"; an actual piece of a Soviet SS-20 missile destroyed under U.S.–Soviet arms accords, fashioned into pins; a leather baseball cap bearing the hammer and sickle logo; a "Free Lithuania" T-shirt; and (startlingly!) radiation counter pins used by Chernobyl clean-up crews – reassuringly described as

Other Influences Loom

One factor bound to have significant impact in the new century was the new fabrics that would become available. One new fabric changed color in response to the wearer's body temperature. Another breakthrough occurred in 1991 when the Du Pont company chemical division announced a new use for their Teflon protective finish, which was previously known for its application to pots and pans. Du Pont announced that, as the finish had fine water and stain repelling qualities, Teflon-coated garments – such as ski parkas, raincoats, uniforms, shorts, shirts, jackets and caps – were being offered for sale by various garment companies.

Long jacket over short skirt, by Rebecca Moses.

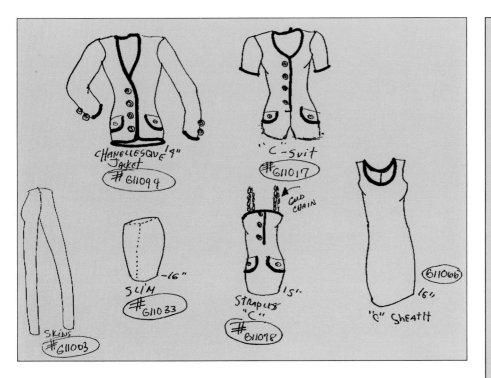

Original designs by Betsey Johnson in black/blue/brown. Skin-tight pants, tightly fitting 16-inch-long mini, a scoop-necked minidress, a sheath dress, two jackets – short and long sleeved – and a strapless fitted minidress, with gold chain "straps" banded in contrasting fabric.

"neutralized, of course." Men could order Soviet field sunglasses and "authentic wool officers coats, complete with hammer/sickle metal buttons, and epaulets" or else a sturdy Soviet worker's jacket. Also "authentic brass Russian military belts" and the "Commandierski" military watch, as worn by Soviet paratroopers.

Men and women could deck themselves out in a number of unusual T-shirts with messages printed in the Cyrillic alphabet. Messages included: Moscow University; CCCP Tank; Siberia – Land of Opportunity; Vodka Is the Enemy of Production; and Sputnik Cowboy. One could also buy T-shirts bearing advertising designs ranging from those promoting the state-run Aeroflot airlines to Ukrainian beets. Men could opt for bi-color drawstring rugby shorts picturing the U.S. flag and the USSR hammer and sickle. Accessories in the catalog also included the shiny metal pins previously used throughout the Soviet Union to reward a job well done or mark events and express political sentiments. To complete the outfit, customers could even purchase an "authentic Soviet flag."

The Designers Speak

American designer Rebecca Moses, noted for her comfortable and elegant designs, told us of her design approach and the look she envisioned for the women of the 1990s. "We have entered a decade of femininity. I'm able to take the classic, easy shapes that I love so much and that are so comfortable to wear and refine them, to dress them up – with color, with texture, with sweet and sexy embellishments. What ends up happening is you get the casualness that *is* American sportswear with a ladylike edge."

America's Betsey Johnson the long-time fashion leader, internationally known for her highly innovative designs, commented that generally speaking for the nineties she

imagined: "Simple, clean, uncontrived, easy and versatile modern clothing . . . I like personal dressing, anything and everything as long as you're happy. The recession has greatly affected everything, especially *retail*, and it's going to continue for a long while, I think. People's priorities are changing with less money . . . buying one [item of clothing] instead of two or three. Designing gets tougher – clothes have to really *mean* something to the customer – they have to be *very* something . . . whatever – to get the customer to part with her money."

American designer Gordon Henderson – winner of the Perry Ellis Young Designer of the Year Award from the Council of Fashion Designers of America – believed that he is challenged to create looks that last, and wanted to change fashion by creating clothes that will stand the test of time. His inspiration was derived from the: "golden era of sportswear design, the fifties . . . a time when American designers had their first real impact on the rest of the fashion world. The American look defined."

While Mr. Henderson was inspired by the past, there was nothing old hat about his stylings. Instead he created streamlined, all-American fashions, derived from the past but revved up

Times Might Be A-Changing

According to estimates, the American populace was aging – and widening! Therefore, where once the only fashions one would see were those suitable for the reed-thin and youthful figure, as the millennium approached companies increasingly began producing fashions for ample-figured women, while others focused upon older customers. Concurrently there was a demand for (what were called) "plus size models," both for live fashion presentations and for photo sessions.

Left: Nightclubbing for all.

Above: Australia's Anneliese Seubert – "Model of the Decade."

with his distinct touch. He commented: "... in the photo archives of the New York Public Library, I found these shapes ... the twin sets, cardigans and car coats, circle skirts, Capri pants, cable knit sweaters, and cheerleader shirts ... they looked so great, so cool for today, translated for the nineties.... The woman I'm designing for has her own sense of style. She doesn't want to be dictated to. She's absolutely free to mix things from my collection anyway she wants. I'm focusing on a feeling, a spirit, rather than a single short or long skirt. I give her the choice. ... In the clubs, in restaurants, shopping, I'm designing for the girl on the street, the working woman ...".

Young New Yorker Isaac Mizrahi was the winner of many prestigious awards, including the 1990 Council of Fashion Designer of the Year Award; 1990's best designer of the Fashion Footwear Association of New York; and cited in *Crain's New York* business [newspaper] in their annual "40 Under 40" award group. After only a few seasons in business Mr. Mizrahi drew splendid notices. Carrie Donovan in the *New York Times Magazine* said of his spring '90 collection: "... practical clothes – carried out in fresh colors and marvelously inventive patterns ... true originality. They are in the American sportswear tradition but with an added layer of young sophistication ... Mizrahi will be the hero of the next decade."

Hold that Pose

As always there was a demand for attractive models. One young woman whose career got off to a roaring start was Australia's Anneliese Seubert, who was chosen to be the USA's "Super Model of the Decade," by the famed Ford Models, Inc. agency, in New York City.

Looking ahead Mr. Joseph Hunter, vice president of the agency, re-marked that the 21st century may well see changes in the printed picturizations of models, through the use of the Sytex computer system that will permit users to "create" a particular look by shifting one model's eyes onto another's face; or one's legs onto another's body.

Fashion photographers have always been on the cutting edge of fashion. The early nineties saw the emergence of new fashion photographers, including the American Steven Meisel. Unlike photographers of the preceding two decades, who only photographed beautiful models, Meisel specialized in reality *and* artifice. He often made surprising choices, as in one advertising campaign for the Italian designers Dolce and Gabanna where he used a short, slightly overweight model. Although best known for his fashion work, Mr. Meisel also gained wide recognition for his provocative, and controversial, portraits of Madonna, and other superstars featured in the American magazines *Vanity Fair, Rolling Stone* and *Interview*. The photographer said he styled and lit his shots in the style of the old Hollywood stills (i.e., non-moving pictures).

Meisel used many effects to create his unique final product. Top model Linda Evangelista remarked that he had even given her a "playful facelift," – tautly pulling her skin with surgical tape and string. Unlike photographers of past generations, who only strove to show picture-perfect beauties, Meisel created startling images. In one such photo, Ms. Evangelista, wearing fishnet gloves, clawed at her (quite magnificent) face. New York art gallery owner James Danziger called Meisel an "anti-beauty fashion photographer." The former art director of Italian *Vogue*, Juan Gatti, said, "there's a sense of death in his pictures, the drive to recreate something that time forgot," Whatever his drive, Meisel's exciting work helped propel Italian *Vogue* to a wide, new audience – and seemed to capture the mood of the new decade.

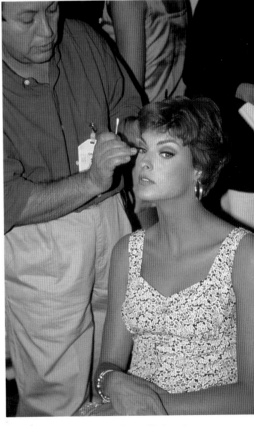

Top model Linda Evangelista at work.

The Pleasure of Leisure

Purely for Leisure

Whereas in the eighties, leisurewear had tended to mean sporty tracksuits and sneakers, in the nineties, the concept broadened to include clothes that could be worn on virtually any occasion, whether informal or at work.

The range of leisurewear was enormous, with anything from "shell-suits" in pastel pinks and blues for both men and women, especially popular in Europe, to sleek Lycra leggings worn with Timberland boots and a chenille "sloppy joe" sweater. Choice was the name of the game.

The recession meant that many people had less money to spend, so difficult-to-wear designer clothes and short-lived high fashion trends tended to lose out to the safer, and generally cheaper, formulas of jeans, leggings, T-shirts and tracksuits.

Dance Energy

The night-clubbing boom showed no signs of letting up, with both music and fashion trends tending to recycle previous styles. Music from Latin America and Africa continued to spice up the Western dance scene. Whatever the style, the emphasis was most definitely on dance music, and this was reflected in the huge variety of easy-to-wear clothes from minimal bra tops and stretch fabric catsuits to loose flowing Indian cotton dresses or pants.

Madonna, dressed by Gaultier.

"Raves" or "warehouse parties" remained popular as well. These were frequently only semi-legal and held in obscure countryside or urban locations, where half the fun was in tracking down the party itself. Fashions at these parties tended toward the practical, with baggy jeans and T-shirts, or Day-Glo surfwear both popular. House music with a high number of beats per minute (bpm), with different tracks often played simultaneously by club DJs, transported dancers into a catatonic state of frenzied movement.

Elements of camp and kitsch were popular fashion themes at New York events such as the Love Ball II, which raised money for AIDS/HIV charities. Cross-dressers parodied supermodels like Naomi Campbell and Linda Evangelista at the infamous London nightclub Kinky Gerlinky; in a logical progression from the "vogueing" of the late eighties, dancers would strike model-like poses. Madonna continued to influence, most recently wearing gold spiraled bra tops and corsets by Jean-Paul Gaultier on her Blonde Ambition tour.

MTV continued to exert a powerful influence on American style, with the dancers on shows such as that hosted by Downtown Julie Brown epitomizing the street style of contemporary leisurewear.

The Retro Scene

Sixties and seventies fashions made a comeback in the nineties. Pop groups such as Deee-Lite and De La Soul turned to sixties psychedelia, now interpreted in Lycra and Spandex instead of the original sweaty polyester and nylon. Wide headbands were popular for all ages, and Mary Quant daisy motifs, beads, medallions and false eyelashes were all widely seen. A-line dresses and baby-doll dresses were worn nineties-style over tight leggings, often in stretch velvet, or with denim cut-offs. U.S. singer Lenny Kravitz, wearing flower power flared pants with bare tattooed torso, played music influenced by Jimi Hendrix and John Lennon.

Fight the Power

Black music was a powerful force in the early nineties. A resurgence of interest in soul and funk emerged parallel to a new direction in rap. The rise of black Hollywood filmmakers like Spike Lee and John Singleton encouraged this trend, with Lee mixing rap with soul in *Do the Right Thing* and with jazz in *Mo' Better Blues*, and the

success of rapper Ice Cube in Singleton's *Boyz 'n the Hood*. Rap was moving away from the raw violence of such groups as NWA (Niggers with Attitude), who weighed themselves down with heavy gold jewelry. Groups such as Public Enemy wrote political lyrics dealing with the struggle in South Africa and urban racism in the U.S. They also attacked perceived barriers in music by touring Europe with the white heavy metal band Anthrax. On stage, gold was abandoned in favor of leather medallions and traditional African fabrics. Rap and hip hop followers wore huge baggy jeans with big patterned shirts and heavy black shoes. Dreadlocks or box-cut and high-top haircuts finished off the look.

Above: Bodysuit for party and club wear by Katherine Hamnett.

Left: Designer TV. MTV style "reporter," superstar model Cindy Crawford, wearing an outfit by Gianni Versace, interviewing Lady Miss Kier, dressed by Thiery Mugler, and Dmitry of the group Deee-Lite.

Clubbers cross-dress at the famous
Kinky Gerlinky club in London.

Downtown Julie Brown.

Stretch-velvet jump suit and a shift
with scroll embroidery by Josie
Natori.

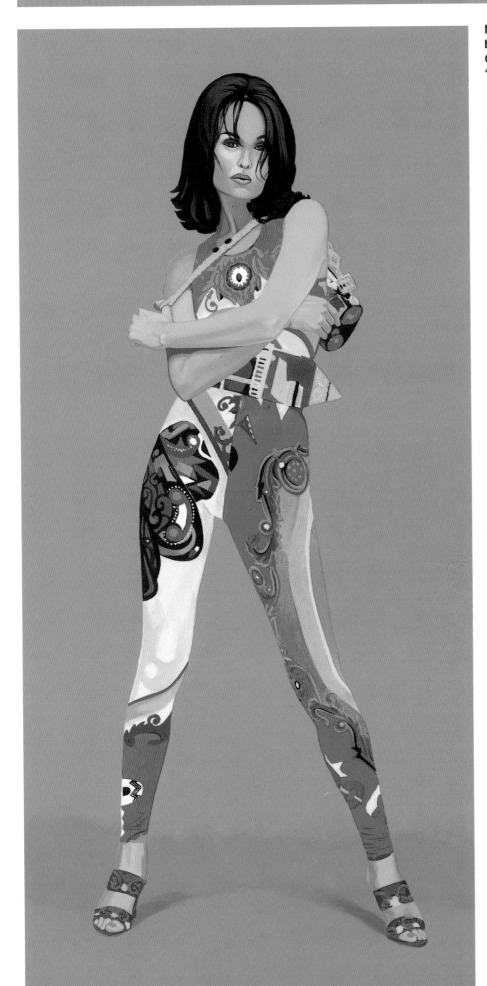

Multicolored Lycra-mix swimsuit
body and Lycra-mix leggings from
Gianni Versace, worn with a wide,
"psychedelic" belt.

Nightclub styles ranged from dyed
hair and costume jewelry to fantasy
creations in leather or latex.

31

Sportswear Gets Active

Stretch to Fit

Some trends continued unchanged from the eighties, and one of these was the ever-increasing popularity of sports and other vigorous forms of exercise – workouts, aerobics, bodybuilding. Special clothing created for these activities continued to grow in popularity, and men and women of all ages had a wide selection from which to choose. Comfort was the byword for all these garments – as was ease of movement in fabrics that stretched easily and yet retained their shape.

Styles continued to evolve, in line with the general direction of eighties fashion, but the preferred fabrics for exercise and sportswear remained Lycra/cotton and Lycra/nylon blends. Several of the eighties styles were interpreted in new ways. For example, under the influence of "rap" style, many men adopted the baseball cap worn with the peak facing backward – or else wore the cap the right way around, but with a ponytail slipped through the fastening at the back of the cap.

The Designer Connection

Meanwhile, sportswear continued to influence the collections of many younger designers. Gordon Henderson delved back into the American past for some of his design ideas – he was described by Patrick McCarthy, executive editor of *Women's Wear Daily*, as the "great synthesizer of American sportswear." Isaac Mizrahi also drew on the traditions of American fashion for collections that the designer himself described as "a kind of hybrid ethnicity. I want my clothing to be as comfortable as a pair of pajamas, but suitable for Wall Street . . . and I want it to be very American in feeling . . ."

Elsewhere, Rifat Ozbek and other European designers were turning to more exotic influences to unify sports and dancewear into a new breed of clubbing and "rave" wear. Ozbek and other young designers in the U.K. mixed up stretch Lycra sports and exercise fabrics with exotic cotton and silk prints from India, Africa and elsewhere to produce a look that maximized the freedom of movement of the sports field with the glamour and surface interest of variegated textures and weaves. Those who took their dancing seriously required all the stretch and cool comfort of sportswear while they "worked out" on the dance floor.

"Cotton essentials" for bodywear and streetwear: a camisole leotard with low racing-back and a 3/4 sleeve leotard with Capri tights from Marika Fitness Apparel.

Work That Body! Easy-to-wear outfits in stretch Lycra from Marika.

Christine Farmer-Patrick made fashion as well as athletic headlines.

Cropped top and cycle shorts fashioned from a nylon/Lycra blend in strong, bright "neon" colors.

New and Old

Sportswear promised to offer a fascinating clash in the nineties between the new and the old. Traditional fabrics such as denim and cotton remained popular – or underwent significant revivals, as part of the general nineties boom in "retro" looks. But active sportswear also raced ahead to embrace the latest in new fabrics and designs. New "microfiber" fabrics, such as Thinsulate and Polartec, were increasingly used in outdoor wear. These materials could provide the warmth of down or other heavy padding without the bulk, making them perfect for new styles of streamlined outerwear. This trend was based not just on fashion, but the real demands of professional sportsmen and sportswomen to gain a competitive edge in their chosen pursuit. Sometimes – as with the record-holding American sprinter Christine Farmer-Patrick – it was hard to tell where competitive sport ended and fashion began.

Ice-T

Bodybuilding!

Above: (Left) Bra top and high-waisted stirrup pants and (right) bodysuit with Capri leggings, from Baryshnikov Sport.

Right: A very "California girl" look – two girls ready to take off on their bicycles, dressed in denim outfits.

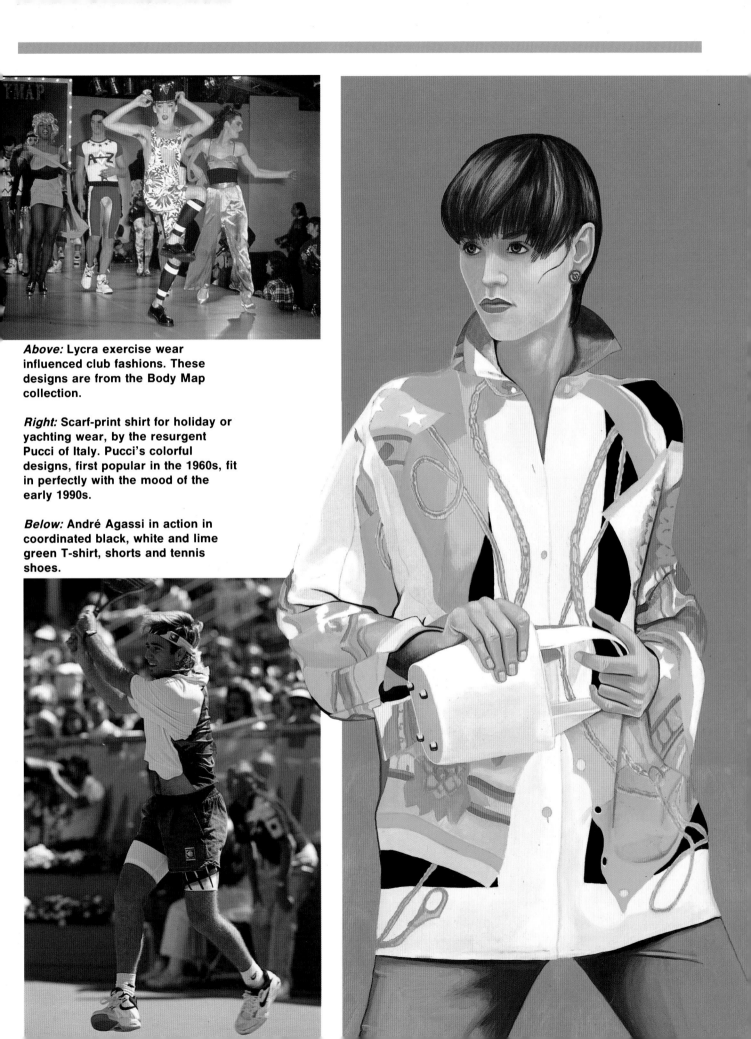

Above: Lycra exercise wear influenced club fashions. These designs are from the Body Map collection.

Right: Scarf-print shirt for holiday or yachting wear, by the resurgent Pucci of Italy. Pucci's colorful designs, first popular in the 1960s, fit in perfectly with the mood of the early 1990s.

Below: André Agassi in action in coordinated black, white and lime green T-shirt, shorts and tennis shoes.

Fashion Goes to Work

Relaxed Office Wear

The working woman of the 1990s had many styles of clothing to choose from for her workaday life. Gone were the days of only one acceptable "look" and one skirt length with possibly one or maybe two colors deemed "suitable." Unlike her 1970s and 1980s "dressed for success" sisters, the nineties woman could express herself in her work wardrobe. In every price range women could find attractive separates, dresses, outerwear, footwear and accessories. Executive women – in certain industries – were no longer strictly bound to wear "copycat" male styles with tailored shirtwaist blouses. They were free to select more feminine outfits – as long as these were held to be appropriate office attire. Some organizations, however, still had unwritten codes for the way their female employees were expected to dress. Tailored workday clothing remained a favorite (and always "safe") choice for many women, but others increasingly experimented with innovative designs for their nine to five lives.

Personal Notes

Women employed in creative fields usually had much more leeway and could dress in more *avant-garde*, individualistic outfits than those in areas like law and finance. However, even those employed in more staid environments, while still bound to "dress in good taste," had a wider range of styles to choose from.

Both bold and subdued colors shared the spotlight, as did fitted and loosely

Fashion goes to work in the streets–a bicycle messenger in sportswear and mask.

A belted, slim fitting, paprika-color cashmere turtleneck dress, shown with a matching long wool coat, printed with bold black patterns. The ensemble typifies the easy-going look chosen by many working women.

constructed garments. More daring women took to updated versions of menswear looks, *but* with a decided nineties twist! Such outfits included masculine cut pants suits, worn with vividly patterned ties; outsize men's watches, and sensible flat heeled men's Oxford tied (or two-toned) shoes and snap brim hats. Designers such as Yohji Yamamoto created oversized menswear-style suit jackets and coordinated trousers. Yves Saint Laurent – in his Rive Gauche collection – showed a striped black and white cotton blend jacket with black silk pants. Italy's designers "followed suit." Romeo Gigli created a silk and linen blend classic men's three-piece navy suit, while Giorgio Armani showed several such outfits – including a black linen jacket and matching trouser pants, and a white silk and linen blend jacket and trouser.

Suits Take on a New Look

Early in the decade, long suit jackets were seen worn with miniskirts – this in both matching and contrasting fabrics and colors. Another variation on suit dressing comprised wearing an unmatched skirt and jacket. Plaids of every type were a huge hit for several seasons and appeared in all manner of apparel and accessories.

Accessories struck a bold note. Women wore interesting combinations of bead necklaces, and there was a spurt of interest in classic handbags – including the 1950s favorite, the "Kelly Bag" – popularized by Princess Grace [née Kelly] of Monaco.

For the non-traditional working woman, this black-and-white open circle print cotton ensemble by Michael Leva for Spiegal features a coordinated zip-front slip dress and shaped zip-front jacket.

The classic navy blazer, updated for the nineties, by Aquascutum.

A decidedly non-traditional bright yellow cotton suit, with interesting collar and neck detailing and a fitted waist, by Hanae Mori.

Oscar de la Renta created the short redingote-style coat in vivid, oversized plaid wool, with fringed detail and jeweled buttons.

A yellow jersey dress and royal blue wool coat by Emanuel Ungaro.

39

 Time Out

Lengths, Fabrics and Silhouettes Vary

At the end of the 19th century, the Victorian era was notable for its fussy, overdesigned formal wear. One hundred years later, as the world headed toward the 21st century, everything had changed. In the 1990s a more personalized expression of dress-up clothing took hold. In addition to classic short and long dresses and gowns, elegantly tailored suits (and pants, jacket and/or coat ensembles) were seen. Evening suits fashioned in rich fabrics with lush details were also popular. Long jackets were paired with miniskirts. Festive, sometimes bejeweled evening sweater outfits were shown. These were usually paired with long or short skirts and/or evening slacks.

Silhouettes included body-fitting chemise dresses and slim sheaths in long and short lengths – as well as loose and fluid, floating styles. Many ultra-full skirts were buttressed by petticoats. Fabrics ranged from shiny satins, plush velvets, slinky metallic-hued lamés, to laces of many types, and also solid and patterned silks and airy chiffons.

Embellishments were particularly popular early in the decade. Dresses, evening suits, and gowns were studded with ''jewels'' (rhinestones, pearls, beads, sequins and so on). Other decorative details ranged from fur and feather trims to ribbons and braidings of gilt cord.

From the USA's Mary Ann Restivo came this navy evening ensemble – a satin swing coat, with matching wool viscose blazer and skirt, all embellished with glittering rhinestones.

Accessories Strike a Bold Note

Glamorous accessories reigned, especially early in the nineties. Women wore giant "chandelier" drop earrings or outsize glittering button earrings. Fake, or faux, jewelry was in, with even wealthier women – mindful of the realities of crime – taking to wearing the many artfully executed creations that closely replicated "real" jewelry. Masses of "pearl" necklaces were seen, as were row-upon-row of glittering chains, and wide bangle bracelets. Gloves, in many lengths and fabrics, were worn by women. Evening bags ranged from small quilted and chain-handled shoulder bags, to miniature, jeweled clutch (hand-held) bags. There was a resurgence of interest in traditional shapes for handbags.

Shoes were often exuberant additions to evening outfits. Some women wore jewel- and metallic-trimmed classic closed toe and heel stylings, while others favored open back, close front and strapped sandals. In 1991 there was a renewed interest in wearing mules (backless shoes) for evening – and even daytime – wear. High (stiletto) heels continued to be the choice of most women, especially younger women. Some on the cutting edge of chic took to wearing platform-soled shoes. For a time wide belts, often encrusted with faux jewels, were also a popular accessory.

Whether one was headed for a school prom, a wedding or an evening at a club, dressing up was in. Unlike the 1970s, where laid back dressing in jeans and possibly a tie-dyed shirt was the last word in hip style, or the yuppie-inspired and conformist eighties, in the nineties many more women and men strove to personalize their special occasion outfits. For some women this meant donning a loose, silk "big shirt" over a velvet cat suit (unitard) or tight-fit, stretch leggings.

Evening Menswear Plays It Safe – for Some

Save for bolder men (often young and the young-at-heart), who experimented wearing non-traditional dress-up outfits, or those who added a colorful vest (or brightly colored cummerbund) to their tuxedo ensemble, by and large formal menswear showed little variation from that of earlier decades. The formally attired nineties man would still be seen in his standard black tuxedo and trouser with black bow tie, subdued tone cummerbund, white shirt and gleaming patent shoes. Or for more formal occasions he might choose the always "correct" cutaway coat and striped trouser.

A satin dress in rich pink with interesting braid and bow detail, from Hanae Mori. The fad for bold jewelry is also in evidence here.

41

Tartan with a twist, by Oscar de la Renta. A fitted plaid jacket is studded with outsize jewels, bordered in jeweled gold braid, and coupled with a short black velvet skirt.

Double-breasted suit with zipper legs and pockets, by John Richmond, teamed with a black shirt by Comme des Garçons and black boots by Jean-Paul Gaultier.

Brightly colored bra, bolero and fringed shorts by Rifat Ozbek, worn over a yellow bodysuit.

Young American designer Christian Francis Roth is inspired by artists of the Surrealist and Dada movements. This witty "Dollar Bill" dress drew particularly wide publicity.

An elegant, yet "throwaway chic," color-blocked, silk outfit from American designer Carmelo Pomodoro.

Proud to Be Me

Big Is Beautiful

Where once every female was supposed to be super slim, 1990s fashions reflected the reality of what the average woman looks like. Many companies offered attractive garments for every occasion for those who were not model-thin.

One American company, Spiegal, was in the forefront, offering a large selection of attractive outfits for the ample-bodied female. This was a wise marketing move as it was estimated early in the decade that in the USA something like 60 percent of women wore size 12 and up. It was further reported that the so-called plus size market was the fastest growing segment of the apparel industry, with annual growth rates of 25–35 percent. Spiegal's Karen Fullem, manager of their "For You" division, said: "Style has nothing to do with size . . . these are vital, successful, style-conscious women, who just happen to be size 14 and up."

No matter the occasion, the full-figured nineties female no longer had to hide beneath voluminous layers of fabric to mask her girth. In the USA many organizations offered these women – and their male counterparts – special activities. One group held monthly "Large Parties," social dances and get-togethers. These functions were not only attended by ample-bodied people but also drew in "normal" weight people as well.

Organizations promoting the civil rights of oversized people acted to prevent prejudicial treatment in the workplace. One such case involved an amply bodied American nurse who was dismissed from her hospital

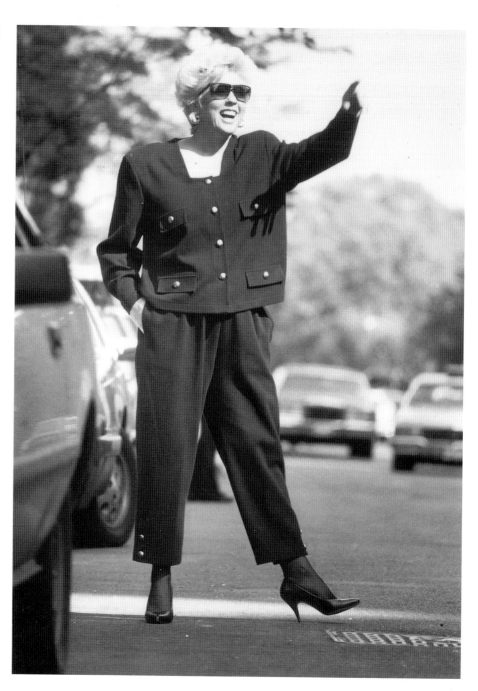

duties due to her weight. She and the organization championing her cause fought the dismissal, citing her excellent work performance and record. These organizations worked to overcome the stereotyping and prejudice associated with overweight.

A black pants suit with gold buttons – a flattering style for any age range.

The fashion community provided increased numbers of styles for the full-figured person.

"Age-ism" and Traditional Beauty

In the 1990s demographic influences played a part in what people wore. The American baby boomers – those born during the period of greatly increased birth rates between 1946 and 1964 – were aging. These baby boomers had affected society and business throughout their lives. Their great numbers brought on the youth culture of the late 1950s and 1960s and now, as they approached middle age, they were leading to other changes in society. Catering to this new generation of women, and men, many designers and manufacturers realized they had to create stylish, yet "age appropriate" clothing. It was surprising to some to realize that even the chic, youthful Princess of Wales turned 30 years old in 1991.

In 1991 Naomi Wolf wrote a best-selling and highly controversial book, *The Beauty Myth: How Images of Beauty Are Used Against Women*. She said that in a society struggling to come to terms with women's changing roles, female beauty, or lack of it, became a "political weapon against women's advancement." Joan Kurianski, executive director of the Older Women's League, concurred stating: "This emphasis on looks is really a disservice to women because it hurts access to employment and how women perceive themselves . . . We need to promote the truth about women." She felt one way to do so was to challenge the negative stereotypes in advertisements and in the media generally, where the ideal woman was pictured as youthful, with flawless skin, a super slim body, and wearing expensive clothes.

Wolf felt that older women: "are more energetic, more powerful, more comfortable" with their abilities, and that: "they need to recognize these qualities and disentangle themselves from the beauty myth." She wrote about the exploitation and obsession fed by a $20 billion a year cosmetics industry, a $33 billion diet industry, a $300 million cosmetic-surgery industry and a $7 billion pornography industry. Not everyone, however, totally agreed with Ms. Wolf.

Camille Paglia, professor of humanities at the University of the Arts in Philadelphia, Pennsylvania said, "Women enjoy color and fabric and fashion and we should not have to apologize for that." Even America's staunch feminist Betty Friedan, writing in *Allure* magazine, argued that it wasn't wrong for feminists to want to be beautiful. "Women could all stop wearing lipstick and blusher, eye shadow and moisturizing cream tomorrow, and I doubt it would help them break through the glass ceiling or get child care or parental leave within the structures of the workplace." The "glass ceiling" refers to the experience of women in business rising just so high in an organization before they "hit a glass ceiling," an unwritten restriction on their further movement up the corporate ladder.

Motherhood no longer means the end of fashion. This one-piece zip-front outfit, with mesh inserts in dazzling white, demonstrates the more adventurous possibilities of clothing for recent mothers.

Bridal wear for the fuller figure can be especially glamorous.

46

A lightweight, one-piece denim jumpsuit for casual wear.

From the popular American design company Liz Claiborne, a reversible bomber jacket and matching shorts, in black-and-white check, worn with a bright yellow T-shirt.

In the nineties, the over-size woman could join her slimmer sisters on the seashore, and do so in extremely flattering beachwear.

A burgundy gown with jeweled front, worn with formal, elbow-length evening gloves.

Eco-Aware

Globally Green

In the 1990s, all across the globe, people became more aware of the fragile nature of the world in which we live. This awareness was widely reflected in both the fashion and cosmetics industries, which began to respond to the consumer's newly awakened desire to be eco-friendly, by emphasizing the ''green-ness'' of their products. Organizations such as Greenpeace promoted themselves through T-shirts and other garments carrying environmental messages.

Animal Rights

Animal rights activists raised loud protests in several fashion-related areas. The fur industry in both Britain and the USA went into decline as shops were attacked and people became too scared to wear their fur coats on the streets, where they might be subject to verbal harassment or even assaulted with spray paint. However, countries such as Italy and Switzerland with a large consumer interest in furs seemed untouched by such protests. Organizations such as LYNX kept the anti-fur lobby going with its effective advertising campaigns and high-profile T-shirts. Fake fur became highly fashionable, although it was wise to stick to the obviously fake rather than run the risk of attack by wearing a more convincing imitation.

greenpeace

"Green" Consumers

"Green" Consumers

In New York and other cities across the United States and in Europe, small eco-friendly stores opened. These stores sold all-natural, undyed and unbleached 100% cotton clothing and linens in response to the demand for such natural fibers and the growing awareness that some types of fabric manufacturing and treating were harmful to the environment. Environmentally safe cleaning and other household products and recycled paper goods were also sold.

These shops, and their customers, recognized that poor undeveloped nations would have problems protecting threatened natural habitats and species unless their people were given ways of supporting themselves other than burning rain forests to farm or poaching endangered animals. Products like Rainforest Crunch, a candy made from nuts grown in the rain forest, made it profitable to protect threatened areas. One store, in Brooklyn, New York, sold jewelry and wallets crafted from discarded tires, giving new life to rubber, which could often be a major environmental headache, and money to people with few ways of earning a living.

As well as the campaign against the slaughter of animals for the sake of fashion, the cosmetics industry came under increasing pressure to abandon the practice of testing its products on live animals. As a result, many companies moved away from concocting synthetic miracle creams in laboratories and began to explore the more natural and traditional ingredients, which would also have appeal under the ''environmentally friendly'' tag. Chain stores such as the Body Shop continued to do well as the demand for cruelty-free products remained buoyant.

Eco-aware clothing from the Greenpeace catalogue.

Endangered Species

In earlier decades, wearing items that incorporated such materials as tortoise shell, ivory or crocodile skin was considered the height of chic. In the nineties, however, such behavior was viewed by growing numbers of people as barbaric. In many nations, the killing of endangered or threatened animals for their skins or the harvesting of elephants for their ivory tusks was prohibited by law. But as long as a market for these products existed, poachers and illegal traders continued to thrive. The problem was exacerbated by the fact that poaching typically occurred in poverty-stricken areas of the world, providing the only means of survival for many people.

Left: Even top couture houses such as Chanel began to introduce fake fur as trimming.

Right: Patricia Field of New York goes one step further: nothing natural was destroyed for this outfit. It's all made of artificial materials, even the wig!

Below: All kinds of fake furs from Luxaire.

Tomorrow's Talent

Witty and Aware

No matter their nationality or training, many up-and-coming fashion designers shared several qualities. The people whose creations are seen here exhibited a witty awareness of the fun that is the essence of fashion, and yet many did so coupled with a sense of the changing needs of 21st century women and men. Many of these designers spoke of the need to allow much more leeway for women to express their individuality through their apparel.

Designing an Identity

New Yorker Sharon Rozsay, trained as a fine artist, is a self-taught designer of custom apparel. Ms. Rozsay bypassed the hustle and frenzy of the city's garment center and sky-high priced Manhattan custom "salon," and she instead located her design studio in a section of downtown Brooklyn overlooking the dazzling New York skyline, a favored location for fine artists. She has had her creations featured in many private shows and sold at a prestigious New York City gallery-shop, Wearable Art. Ms. Rozsay stated: "Fashion is an expansion of one's inner identity." She said that as we approach the new century, "As new directions impact our lives clothing must respond accordingly." Ms. Rozsay felt that designers are increasingly recognizing that they can no longer dictate what is "*the* one look," and that they must allow women to express themselves through their clothing. The pictured creations embody Ms. Rozsay's philosophy.

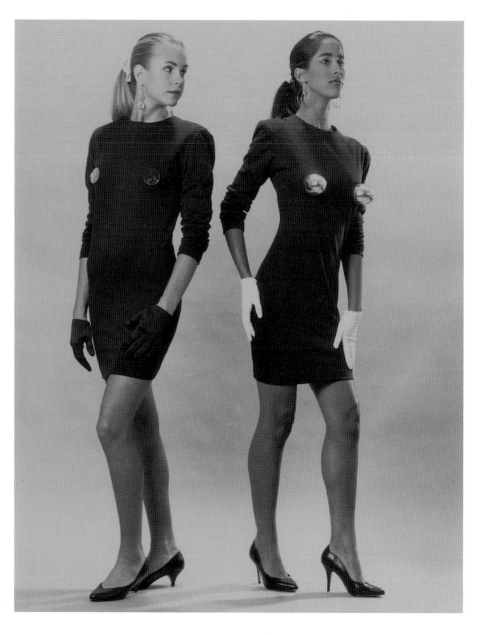

New York City's Parsons School of Design – with a student body drawn from across the globe – has traditionally produced some of the world's most notable designers. A group of award-winning 1990s students' hand-executed creations typifies the reason for the school's fine reputation. Several of the student-designers commented on their work and concepts for what the coming decade – and the future – holds.

New Yorker Sarah Tsang said, "fabrics will be used in different ways, with new synthetics often dictating the shape of garments. Increased feedback from customers will make for more wearable clothing."

Daniela Sarmento, from Brazil, said she is "enamored of textures and plain shapes, and wanted [for one design competition] to weave a jacket that looked like a carpet." Working under the tutelage of American designer Isaac Mizrahi she recalled his highly unusual suggestion: "Get a glass of wine, go to a ribbon store and go crazy!" She bought 28 different ribbons, made of fur, satin, velvet, braid, fake fur, marabou feathers, pom poms and rope and wove them together. The result was her lush, richly textured jacket, pictured here.

Jorge Boan, of New Orleans, Louisiana, remarked, "I think that up to the year 2000 many fashions will be 'retro' stylings, [we will also see] new fabrics and approaches made later in the nineties. Retailing and promotion will [additionally] be affected, I think the smaller designer/manufacturer will [increasingly] own their own shops."

Left: Two polyester/cotton blend black evening dresses by Mariela E. Torres. Both are close fitting, with long sleeves and slightly padded shoulders, each is back zipped. The dress on the left bears mirrored discs and that on the right has enlarged silver "bullet" detailing.

Daniela Sarmento's unusual thickly textured hand-made jacket, worn over a simple black unitard.

***Below:* Christianita Testamark's princess-line fluorescent orange dress in 100 percent cotton knit.**

Projecting the Future

Mariela E. Torres, a fashion student at Daytona Beach Community College, in Florida, felt that the fashions of the decade would "Reflect society's need for simplicity and versatility, yet always express [the wearer's] individuality. Also, "basic, no frills styles are a must . . . we are concerned with saving our lives and our planet . . . conservation is key. Back to earth colors . . . basic black, white, brown, rust and navy. Materials like plastic, metal, wood and glass are being incorporated into fashion [for] an industrial touch." Ms. Torres's projections include: "short skirts, body curving dresses as well as loose fitting, trapeze-shaped, swing style dresses, big over small, . . . tunics worn over slim skirts or shorts," and also continued interest in items such as bustiers. She created a bra adorned with beer caps with an old fashioned style garter belt, which was worn over biker shorts. Ms. Torres also favored gloves, 1960s style wide headbands and the use of fake furs. "I'm constantly experimenting with new fabrics and unusual materials. Plastics are great . . . fashion is a vision . . . it can be whatever you want it to be."

Christianita Testamark, a fashion student at Howard University in Washington, D.C. felt that in the nineties "Fashions will be beautiful and sassy and bring out all the positive qualities in a person."

Mariela E. Torres designed this clear plastic tunic dress with black trim and garters front and back.

Inset: London's Georgia Robinson, designing for the Movements label, created these vivacious outfits of panné velvet pants and tunic tops in stretch-velvet, over sleek leggings and midriff-tied blouses in Indian cottons.

Two designs by students from St. Martins College, London, using natural and organic forms for futuristic designs.

Sharon Rozsay's gold-embroidered lace "bubble," trimmed in satin, encases a slim, color-matched slip dress. The bubble has Indian bead trim at its neckline.

Time of Your Life

Options

No longer bound by strict rules of fashion, people in the 1990s had a myriad of clothing options. The wide availability and popularity of fashion magazines and the rapid transmission of the latest "looks" via television – and also of rock music videos – sped fashion information across the globe.

Melissa Sones, a contributing editor to the American magazine *Mirabella* commented: "Fashion used to filter down from the aristocracy to the average woman . . . but today the so-called aristocracy has changed . . . while fashion still comes from the runways, we *also* have other influences: from the streets, from MTV, from rock and roll music, from films and from a multitude of things going on around us. . . . Exercise has been a big influence. Women began wearing their exercise clothing on the streets, so that it not only became acceptable to do so, but it bred a wide gamut of new leisure wear styles."

Fashion from Everywhere

Street styles continued to have a major influence on fashion. Top among these influences was the style of those who played and listened to rap music. Whereas in the 1980s rap style had consisted mainly of high-priced sneakers and a lot of heavy gold jewelry, in the 1990s it moved in a new direction. Rappers turned away from gold and expensive running shoes in an attempt to downplay the materialism that they saw as having a direct link to urban violence and

Above: Hanae Mori's printed georgette silk dress in black, with white organza bows and huge button earring.

Right: From Mary Ann Restivo, a houndstooth check wool blazer in black, bordeaux, olive and gold, with crossover cable stitch wool sweater, and olive wool crêpe trouser.

crime. Young people in certain neighborhoods had literally been killed over gold chains and top-of-the-line sneakers, and those who could afford to buy them were often drug dealers. Instead of gold, rappers of the 1990s wore leather medallions, often featuring Africa in a combination of red, green, black and yellow – colors associated with African nationalism or Rastafarianism. These looks made their way into mainstream fashion, just as the earlier rap look had.

Another street-originated style that remained popular was the black leather motorcycle jacket. These jackets were worn by men and women of all ages and living all lifestyles. Sometimes they were even worn over suits or evening dresses.

Headcoverings

Headscarves tightly wound about the head in the manner of the 1950s and the 1960s were popular. Other women chose traditional hat styles, including those with wide and narrow brims, men's inspired fedoras, turbans and berets jauntily perched to the side.

More *avant-garde* stylings appealed to those seeking something newer. Head wraps of varied kinds in prints and novelty fabrics were seen. Some women artfully tied lengths of fabric about their heads in interesting ways. The American designer Isaac Mizrahi paid tribute in creating just such head wraps: one in homage to the late Paris designer of the 1950s Jacques Fath; another to actress Lucille Ball when she appeared on *I Love Lucy*, the hit TV show of the same era; and another inspired by the prima ballerina Natalia Makarova.

Of Shoes and Jewels

Footwear, handbags and accessories of all types remained important finishing touches. Some women wore large, bold costume jewelry, while others selected classic, petite jewelry pieces. Save for the reappearance, early in the era, of the platform shoe, most 1990s shoe fashions were in the fairly traditional mode. Women could select from a large number of shoe styles for business or social occasions: comfortable, low-heeled walking shoes; stiletto heels; mid-range heel-heights executed in varied leathers, suedes and fabrics. The freedom afforded by running shoes helped propel them into a "must have" for women of every age and lifestyle.

Goodbye to Stodgy Fashions

Often with nary a nod to the fashion "experts," people thumbed their nose at "style" and wore what pleased them most. One could attend a play, opera or ballet in any of the world's major cities and see elegantly dressed couples seated next to casually (often highly individualistically) attired folk. Dress-up knit sweaters (and T- and

sweatshirts), some glittering with sequins, fur trim, or shiny embellishments, were popular early in the decade. Metallic fabrics of silver and gold were also widely shown in this period.

Much to the relief of Western women, quite a few major designers cleverly bypassed the seasonal quandary of the hemline, in 1991, by showing what were called "long over short" garments. These ranged from graceful, billowy skirts worn over body-tight, short shorts; or long, (front or side) slit, skirts or dresses, worn over miniskirts. A variation on this theme was that of short over tight, as in sleek leggings worn with super short skirts.

Sheer, "see through" fabrics gained a following, particularly among the firm and fit, those eager to show their trim bodies. Some designers created sheer, see-through blouses and dress tops. They were most often shown with skimpy – albeit modest – bras beneath.

Some People Never "Dressed!"

The nineties offered many people the freedom to dress as they pleased. For some, whose lifestyle permitted it, this meant *always* wearing casual clothing. There were large numbers of people who chose to wear casual, easy fitting, comfortable clothing. All over the world young people, and also those who were not so young, wore jeans, and so-called work out clothes (derived from exercise garb) or T- or sweatshirts. Some men gave up dress shirts and ties completely in favor of more relaxed attire. Denim jeans were seen everywhere for almost every occasion, save for the most formal. Some canny designers created dress-up denim wear. People of all ages whose lives necessitated they dress in a traditional manner for business chose these casual outfits for most of their leisure time activities.

Some nineties men bravely returned to brightly colored vests.

Scaasi designed this sweeping bright green ball gown. Perfect for the special occasion at any time of life.

Above: This group of Ford Agency models shopping on Los Angeles's famed Rodeo Drive show some of the varied clothing options open to women today.

Below: "Rave" styles in silver/blue from Vivienne Westwood.

Choices might mean a bright, Pucci-inspired blazer and matching headscarf.

59

Glossary

Anorak Waist-length, hooded jacket, usually with zipper front and drawstring hem, made of water-repellent fabric, frequently fur-lined.

Avant-garde Emerging or newest fashions and/or ideas. French for "vanguard".

Bandeau A bra-like or band-shaped top.

Bangle Bracelet Round, rigid bracelet.

Basque Bodice Fitted bodice, forming inverted "V" where skirt joins the bodice. Frequently seen on formal wear, especially bridal and bridesmaid's dresses.

Bloomers Very loose pants, knee gathered. Named for the 19th-century feminist Amelia Bloomer. She thought it silly that women should wear skirts for sports activities and suggested they wear these garments.

Bodysuit One-piece fitted garment combining bodice and abbreviated panty, without legs, sometimes with snap closing at the crotch.

Bomber Jacket Waist length, bloused style, frequently made of leather, first worn by the USA's armed forces' fliers in World War II. Also known as "flight jackets". Today, worn by men and women.

Bustier Strapless, tight-fitting, longline bra, reaching to the waist, frequently front-closed. Popularized as outerwear by Madonna.

Capri Pants Three-quarter length, tight fitting pants, named for Italian island where they first became popular.

Chemise Straight-lined dress with no waistband, worn unbelted.

Couture Design/manufacture of, high priced, high fashion clothing. Abbreviation of the French phrase, *haute couture*. Originally used to describe custom-made clothing, recently also used to describe fine designer creations, produced in limited quantity.

Cummerbund Wide, pleated, hooked, sash belt. Usually in satin, worn by men with formal wear. Also worn by women with varied outfits.

Cutaway Men's formal coat, usually black, with one button closure, with "skirt" cut away from the waist, forming long tails in back.

Dart Tapering, stitched tuck in a garment.

Dirndl Worn originally by Tyrolean women, peasant skirts which are slightly full in cut and gathered into a waistband.

Faille Closely woven fabric with a slight sheen and barely distinct ribbing.

Gazar A silk fabric, loosely constructed, has a stiffness providing body.

Gore A tapering or triangular skirt section.

Grommet Metal eyelet, mainly used on belts although also seen on hems, cuffs, etc.

Intarsia On knitwear, a design knitted into only certain sections—such as neckband, cuffs or collar.

Harem Pants Loose trousers, gathered into ankle bands.

Houndstooth A broken check pattern woven into varied fabrics.

Jacquard Fabrics with a woven or knitted pattern. Named for Frenchman, Jean Marie Jacquard, c. 1752–1834, inventor of the Jacquard loom; the first machine to weave in patterns.

Jumpsuit One piece suit of shirt and ankle-length pants, usually with a zipper-front, with either long or short sleeves. Worn originally by the military: World War I fliers, in WW II by parachute jumpers and fliers.

Lamé Fabric—wholly or partially—woven or knitted with metallic yarn.

Leotard Tight-fitting, one-piece, stretchable garment, with or without sleeves, reaches from neck to crotch, has no legs. First worn by dancers and acrobats. Named for creator: Jules Léotard, French, 19th-century trapeze artist.

Lycra Trade name for Du Pont Company's version of sturdy, non-rubber, elastic fiber. Also known as Spandex.

Maribou Soft and fluffy feathers, originally those of a wild African stork—now on many nations' list of endangered species. Today usually made of dyed turkey feathers.

Matte Jersey Low luster, dull surfaced fabric, usually cut on the bias to maximize fabric's clinging properties.

Oxfords Laced and tied flat heeled shoes.

Panné Velvet Velvet fabric with pile pressed flat in one direction, creating a shimmering effect.

Pom Pom Round, ball-shaped trim, cut from ends of yarn.

Raglan Sleeve Seamed diagonally from neckline to underarm. Named for Lord Raglan, British commander who led the Crimean War's Charge of the Light Brigade.

Redingote Thought to be a shortened form of "riding coat," a full princess-line coat, classically styled with no fastening beneath waistline in order to show the garment worn beneath.

Retro Prefix meaning backward—used to describe items inspired by those of earlier time periods.

Tartan From Scotland, plaid pattern denoting specific clan. Authentic tartan plaids must be so approved by the Lyon Court in Edinburgh, Scotland, be registered and have a name assigned.

Tortoise Shell Brownish-yellow, semi-transparent, mottled turtle shell. Once popular (now banned in the USA), for combs, jewelry, ornaments, decorative objects, etc. Faux tortoise shell is now often made from plastic.

Unitard One-piece, tight-fitting bodysuit, reaching from neck and/or shoulders to ankles, combined leotard with long-legged, tights, sometimes with stirrup straps fitted under foot's instep.

Velour Soft, dense-pile, velvet knit or woven fabric.

Voile Lightweight, simply woven, semi-transparent fabric of cotton, silk, or synthetic material.

Reading list

Few books have yet been published exclusively on nineties fashion. However, many earlier publications will give useful historical insights into the contemporary trend of events. Fashion's future grows out of its past. Magazines are always the best source of information on the current scene.

Adult General Reference Sources
Black, J.A., Garland, M. and Kennett, F., *A History of Fashion* (Orbis, 1975).
Calasibetta, Charlotte, *Essential Terms of Fashion; A Collection of Definitions* (Fairchild, 1985).

Calasibetta, Charlotte, *Fairchild's Dictionary of Fashion*, 2nd Edition (Fairchild, 1988).
Cassini, Oleg, *In My Own Fashion* (Simon & Schuster, 1987).
De La Haye, Amy, *Fashion Sourcebook* (Wellfleet Press, 1988).
Fairchild, John, *Chic Savages* (Simon & Schuster, 1989).
Fraser, Kennedy, *Scenes from the Fashionable World* (Knopf, 1987).
Gold, Annalee, *90 Years of Fashion* (Fairchild, 1990).
O'Hara, Georgina, *The Encyclopedia of Fashion* (Harry N. Abrams, 1986).
Schurnberger, Lynn, *Let There Be Clothes* (Workman, 1991).

Steele, Valerie, *Paris Fashion: A Cultural History* (OUP, 1988).
Steele, Valerie, *Women of Fashion; 20th Century Designers* (Rizzoli, 1990).
Stegemeyer, Anne, *Who's Who in Fashion* (Fairchild, 1988).
Trahey, Jane (ed.), *100 Years of the American Female from Harper's Bazaar* (Random House, 1967).

Young Adult Sources
Ruby, Jennifer, *The Nineteen Eighties* (David & Charles, 1991).
Wilcox, R. Turner, *Five Centuries of American Costume* (Scribner's, 1963).

Acknowledgments

The Author and Publishers would like to thank the following for permission to reproduce illustrations: Allsport for page 33a; Aquascutum for page 38b; Janet Boyes for page 55a and c; Cedars-Erez for page 10; Oscar de la Renta for pages 38c and 42; Miguel Dominguez for page 29; Duggal Colour Projects for page 26b; Louis Feraud for pages 16 and 17a; Ford Model for page 58-9; Gamma for pages 8–9 and 11; Gantos for page 14; Greenpeace for pages 48–49; Betsey Johnson for page 25; Kimberley Johnson for page 53b; Norma Kamali for page 21a and b; LA Gear/Heather Rem for page 34d; Dan Lecca/Rebecca Moses for page 24; Link-Up for page 33b; Maury Rogoff Public Relations for pages 32, 33c and 45; Isaac Mizrahi for page 19a and b; Hanae Mori for pages 36b, 38a, 41 and 56; Movements in Fashion for pages 20 and 54b; Prisma Fotogiornalismo for page 18; Mary Ann Restivo for pages 40 and 57; Rex Features for the frontispiece and pages 6b, 22a, 22b, 23a, 26a, 27b, 28, 29b, 30a, 31b, 31c, 35a, 35b, 36a, 43b and 59a; Daniel Sarmento for page 53b; Arnold Scaasi for pages 7 and 58b; SIPA Press for pages 6a, 15, 17b and 23b; George Smith: Photographer for page 43a; Spiegal Inc. for pages 37a, 43b, 44, 47a, 47b, 47c; Everett Tolley for page 12; Mariela Torres for page 52. The illustrations were researched by David Pratt. Special thanks are due to Lighthorne Pictures and Naked City Pictures for their cooperation in preparing the material used on pages 28–29, 40–41, 48–49 and 60–62.

"WE HAVE ENTERED A DECADE OF FEMININITY"

"I THINK THAT UP TO THE YEAR 2000 FASHION WILL BE 'RETRO' STYLES"

"I'M CONSTANTLY EXPERIMENTING WITH NEW FABRICS AND UNUSUAL MATERIALS"

"SEXY, AND SASSY!"

"THE JAPANESE ARE HUNGRY FOR A CERTAIN KIND OF AMERICANA"

"ANYTHING AND EVERYTHING AS LONG AS YOU'RE HAPPY"

"FALSE OPTIMISM WILL BE THE HALLMARK OF THE DECADE"

"I'M FOCUSING ON A FEELING, A SPIRIT, RATHER THAN A SINGLE SHORT OR LONG SKIRT"

"IT'S GLOBALIZATION!"

"GET A GLASS OF WINE, GO TO A RIBBON STORE AND GO CRAZY!"

"JUST BECAUSE A WOMAN DOESN'T HAVE THE POCKETBOOK . . ."

". . . THAT DOESN'T MEAN SHE DOESN'T HAVE STYLE"

Darlexx – more familiar as a material to scuba divers than fashion designers – was used by Pamela Dennis to style this zipper-decorated black minidress.

Index

Note: numbers in *italics* refer to illustrations